Mastering
CRUD

with Flask in 5 Days;

Build Python Web Applications - From Novice to Pro

Level Up Your Skills with a Flask & Python Web Development Blueprint Crash Course

MARK JOHN P. LADO, MIT

ISBN: 9798308279174

Imprint: Independently published

DEDICATION

This book is dedicated to all the passionate developers, dreamers, and problem-solvers who believe in the power of technology to transform ideas into impactful solutions.

To the beginners embarking on their first journey into web development, may this guide serve as your compass, illuminating the path of learning and discovery. To the seasoned programmers seeking simplicity in complexity, may you find this resource a reminder of the elegance in foundational tools like Flask and SQLite.

To the educators who inspire curiosity and the students who relentlessly pursue understanding—this book is for you. Your commitment to growth and your unwavering determination to create and innovate push the boundaries of what's possible in the digital world.

A special acknowledgment goes to the open-source community, whose collective knowledge and collaborative spirit make learning and building accessible to everyone. This book would not exist without your contributions.

Finally, to those who dare to dream big and turn concepts into creations, may this book fuel your passion, spark new ideas, and remind you that every line of code has the potential to change the world.

Thank you for being part of this journey. Let's create, learn, and grow—together.

ACKNOWLEDGMENTS

Creating this book would not have been possible without the support, guidance, and inspiration of many individuals and communities.

First and foremost, I would like to thank the open-source community, whose collaborative spirit and contributions to tools like Flask and SQLite have been invaluable. Your passion and dedication to sharing knowledge are the foundation of this work.

To my family and friends, thank you for your unwavering encouragement and patience throughout this journey. Your belief in my vision has been a source of strength.

I am also deeply grateful to the educators, mentors, and colleagues who have shaped my understanding of web development. Your insights and teachings have left a lasting impact.

Finally, to my readers—thank you for placing your trust in this book. Your curiosity and determination to learn are what drive me to create resources like this. This is for you.

TABLE OF CONTENTS

This page is intentionally left blank

CHAPTER 1.

INTRODUCTION

Python has become a favored language for web development due to its simplicity and versatility, and Flask, a micro web framework, is often the go-to choice for developers who prefer lightweight and efficient solutions. When combined with SQLite, a self-contained, serverless, and zero-configuration database engine, Flask can be utilized to perform CRUD operations with exceptional ease. CRUD, which stands for Create, Read, Update, and Delete, represents the four basic functions of persistent storage and is essential for building any dynamic application.

In the context of web applications, CRUD operations allow users to interact with the database, enabling functionalities like adding new data, retrieving existing data, modifying data, and removing data. Flask provides a straightforward way to implement these operations by using its built-in routing and request handling capabilities. The process begins with setting up a Flask application and then connecting it to an SQLite database. This connection is typically established by using Python's `sqlite3` module, which provides a robust interface to interact with the SQLite database directly from the Flask application.

The creation of new entries in the database is facilitated through the 'Create' operation. In a Flask application, this usually involves defining a route that handles POST requests containing the data to be stored. Once the data is received, it is inserted into the SQLite database using SQL commands executed within a Flask view function. Flask's seamless integration with HTML templates allows developers to render forms that collect user input, making the creation of new data intuitive and user-friendly.

Reading from the database, or the 'Read' operation, is equally straightforward. Flask allows for the creation of routes that respond to GET requests, fetching data from the SQLite database and then presenting it to the user. This data retrieval is typically done by executing SQL SELECT statements within the view function and passing the results to a template for rendering. This process enables developers to display lists of records, search results, and detailed views of individual records in a web application.

Updating existing database records, represented by the 'Update' operation, involves selecting the record to be modified and then executing an SQL UPDATE statement. In Flask, this is often achieved by creating a route that processes PUT or POST requests, containing the new data for the selected record. The data is then updated in the database, and the user is often redirected to a page showing the updated information, ensuring a smooth user experience.

Finally, the 'Delete' operation allows for the removal of records from the database. This operation is typically handled by defining a route in Flask that responds to DELETE requests. The route executes an SQL DELETE command to remove the specified record from the SQLite database, allowing users to manage and maintain the data effectively.

In summary, using Flask with SQLite to perform CRUD operations is an efficient method to manage data in web applications. Flask's simplicity and SQLite's lightweight nature make them ideal for developers who seek to build dynamic, data-driven applications quickly and with minimal overhead. With the power of Python, implementing these operations becomes not only straightforward but also a flexible solution for various application needs.

1.1 CRUD: THE BACKBONE OF DATA MANIPULATION

CRUD (Create, Read, Update, Delete) operations are the bedrock of persistent data management in virtually all web applications and many other software systems. They define the basic actions that can be performed on stored data, providing a standardized interface for interacting with databases. The "Create" operation corresponds to inserting new records into a database table. For instance, when a user registers on a social media platform, a new record is created in a "users" table, storing their username, password (hashed for security), email, and other relevant information. This process often involves input validation and sanitization to prevent security vulnerabilities like SQL injection (OWASP, 2021). The "Read" operation retrieves data from the database. In an e-commerce setting, browsing a product catalog triggers "Read" operations to fetch product details (name, description, price, images) from a "products" table and display them to the user. This can involve complex queries with filtering, sorting, and pagination for efficient data retrieval (Silberschatz et al., 2010). "Update" modifies existing records. If a user changes their profile picture or updates their shipping address, an "Update" operation modifies the corresponding record in the "users" table. Implementing proper concurrency control mechanisms, such as optimistic or pessimistic locking, is crucial to prevent data corruption when multiple users attempt to update the same record simultaneously (Bernstein & Newcomer, 1997). Finally, "Delete" removes records. When a user deletes their account or an administrator removes an outdated product listing, a "Delete" operation removes the corresponding record from the database. This operation often requires careful consideration of data integrity and referential constraints to avoid orphaned records. For example, if a customer is deleted, their orders should either be deleted as well or reassigned to a default user. A common question is how CRUD relates to HTTP methods. Typically, "Create" maps to POST, "Read" to GET, "Update" to PUT or PATCH, and "Delete" to DELETE. Understanding CRUD is essential for building robust and functional applications, as it provides a clear framework for managing data persistence across various domains, from simple to-do lists to complex enterprise systems.

1.2 WHY FLASK? A LIGHTWEIGHT AND PYTHONIC CHOICE

Flask, a microframework for Python, offers a compelling solution for developing CRUD (Create, Read, Update, Delete) applications due to its lightweight nature, flexibility, and Pythonic design. Unlike full-stack frameworks that impose a rigid structure, Flask provides a minimalist core, giving developers fine-grained control over their application's architecture. This is particularly advantageous for smaller projects or when performance is a critical concern, as it avoids the overhead of unnecessary features. For instance, consider building a RESTful API for managing a library's book catalog. Flask's lightweight nature allows developers to focus specifically on the API endpoints for creating, retrieving, updating, and deleting book records, minimizing bloat. This resonates with the Unix philosophy of "doing one thing and doing it well" (Raymond, 2003).

Flask's flexibility stems from its microframework philosophy. It provides the essential tools for routing, request handling, and templating, but allows developers to choose external libraries for specific functionalities like database interaction (e.g., SQLAlchemy for relational databases or MongoDB for NoSQL databases), authentication (e.g., Flask-Login, OAuthlib), and form handling (e.g., WTForms). This "batteries included but removable" approach empowers developers to tailor their application to precise requirements. For example, a social media application built with Flask could leverage Flask-Login for user authentication, a NoSQL database for handling user posts, and a message queue like Redis for real-time notifications. This modularity promotes code reusability and maintainability. A common question arises about how Flask handles database interactions. Flask itself does not include a database abstraction layer; instead, it encourages integration with external libraries like SQLAlchemy (Bayer, 2023), an Object Relational Mapper (ORM) that provides a high-level interface for interacting with relational databases. This separation of concerns allows developers to choose the database technology that best suits their needs.

Finally, Flask's Pythonic nature makes it easy to learn and use for developers familiar with Python. Its clean syntax and adherence to Pythonic conventions contribute to more readable and maintainable code. The framework's documentation is also well-regarded, providing clear examples and explanations. This ease of use translates to faster development cycles and reduced learning curves, especially for those transitioning from other Python-based projects. The to-do list example illustrates this perfectly: a simple CRUD application can be implemented in a few lines of Python code using Flask, demonstrating its simplicity and efficiency.

1.3 WHY SQLITE? SIMPLE AND SELF-CONTAINED

SQLite, a self-contained, serverless, zero-configuration, transactional SQL database engine, plays a vital role in simplifying data persistence for various applications, especially those employing CRUD operations. Its key strengths lie in its simplicity, file-based nature, and serverless architecture. The "simple" aspect of SQLite refers to its ease of setup and use. Unlike traditional client-server RDBMS like PostgreSQL or MySQL, SQLite requires no separate server process. The entire database resides within a single file on the host file system. This drastically reduces administrative overhead, making it an excellent choice for rapid prototyping, small-scale applications, and embedded systems (Hipp, 2023). For example, a student developing a desktop application for managing personal finances could easily integrate SQLite without needing to install and configure a database server. This addresses a common concern for beginners who might find setting up complex database systems daunting.

SQLite's file-based nature offers significant advantages in terms of portability and deployment. The entire database, including tables, indexes, and data, is contained within a single file. This file can be easily copied, moved, and backed up, simplifying deployment and data sharing. This is particularly useful in scenarios where applications need to be deployed on different platforms or distributed as standalone packages. Consider a mobile application that stores user data locally. Using SQLite, the database file can be bundled within the application package, ensuring data persistence even when the device is offline. This portability also facilitates testing and debugging, as developers can easily share database files for reproducing issues. A frequent question is how SQLite handles concurrency. Since it's file-based, it uses file locking to manage concurrent access. While this approach is suitable for many applications, it can become a bottleneck under high concurrency scenarios. For applications expecting a large number of concurrent write operations, a client-server RDBMS might be a more appropriate choice (Kreps et al., 2011).

The "no server" characteristic of SQLite further simplifies its deployment and reduces resource consumption. It eliminates the need for a separate server process, reducing memory footprint and CPU usage. This makes it ideal for resource-constrained environments like embedded systems, mobile devices, and IoT devices. For instance, a sensor collecting data in a remote location could use SQLite to store the readings locally, minimizing power consumption and storage requirements. This also simplifies application development as there is no need to manage client-server communication. The to-do list application example effectively demonstrates SQLite's suitability for simple data storage needs. Creating tables for tasks, descriptions, and status within a single file provides a straightforward and efficient way to persist application data.

1.4 PROJECT SETUP: GETTING YOUR HANDS DIRTY

Building a CRUD Application with Flask and SQLite

Now that we've explored the fundamental concepts of CRUD operations, Flask web framework, and SQLite database, let's dive into setting up a basic Flask project to manage tasks using CRUD. This hands-on example will provide a practical understanding of these concepts working together.

1. **Project Setup:**

   o **Create a project directory:**

   ```
   mkdir task_manager
   cd task_manager
   ```

   o **Install Flask and sqlite3 libraries:** Use pip to install the required libraries:

   ```
   pip install Flask sqlite3
   ```

- o **Create a requirements.txt file (optional):** While optional, creating a requirements.txt file is a recommended practice for dependency management. It lists all the project's dependencies in a text file. You can create an empty one now using:

```
touch requirements.txt
```

Later, add Flask and sqlite3 to this file for easy sharing and reproducibility. This ensures anyone can recreate your project's environment by simply running pip install -r requirements.txt.

2. **Project Structure:**

A well-organized project structure promotes maintainability and collaboration. Here's a recommended structure for your Flask CRUD application:

task_manager/

    app.py (main Flask application file)

    models.py (defines database models)

    views.py (handles user requests and interacts with models)

13

templates/ (folder to hold HTML templates for the user interface)

- o app.py: This is the core Flask application file that initializes the Flask instance, configures routes, and ties everything together.

- o models.py: This file defines the data models representing your database tables (e.g., Task model for storing task details).

- o views.py: This file handles user requests (typically routed through URLs), interacts with the database models to perform CRUD operations (Create, Read, Update, Delete tasks), and prepares data to be rendered in templates.

- o templates/: This folder holds the HTML templates that define the application's user interface (UI). Flask uses these templates to dynamically generate web pages based on user interaction and data retrieved from the database.

Separating these functionalities promotes code reusability, improves readability, and makes it easier to maintain the application as it grows in complexity.

Addressing User Questions:

- **Alternative database choices?** While SQLite is a great choice for simple applications, for larger-scale projects with high concurrency or complex data models, consider using a client-server database like PostgreSQL or MySQL. These offer features like ACID transactions (Atomicity, Consistency, Isolation, Durability) for robust data integrity and scalability for handling a larger number of users and data volume (Garcia-Molina et al., 2002).

- **UI frameworks for Flask?** Flask is a lightweight framework, and you can choose additional libraries to build your UI. Bootstrap is a popular option for creating responsive web interfaces (https://getbootstrap.com/).

- **Deployment considerations?** Once your application is developed, you can deploy it on various platforms. Popular options include Heroku (https://www.heroku.com/) for cloud deployment and Apache for web server deployment (https://httpd.apache.org/).

This step-by-step guide provides a solid foundation for building CRUD applications with Flask and SQLite. By following these steps and addressing the mentioned considerations, you can develop functional and maintainable web applications.

Chapter 2.

Database Setup

Databases are fundamental to modern web applications, providing persistent storage for application data. They enable applications to store, retrieve, update, and delete information efficiently and reliably. This section explores the crucial role of databases in web applications, focusing on key concepts and practical considerations.

Importance of Databases:

Web applications often need to store various types of data, including user accounts, product catalogs, transactional data, and application settings. Databases provide a structured and organized way to manage this data, ensuring data integrity, consistency, and efficient access. Without databases, applications would struggle to manage large amounts of data effectively, leading to data loss, inconsistencies, and performance issues.

Types of Databases:

Several types of databases are commonly used in web applications:

- **Relational Databases (SQL):** These databases organize data into tables with rows and columns, establishing relationships between tables using foreign keys. Examples include MySQL, PostgreSQL, SQLite, and Oracle. They are well-suited for applications with structured data and complex relationships. The relational model, formalized by Codd (1970), provides a strong foundation for data integrity and consistency.

- **NoSQL Databases:** These databases offer flexible data models that do not adhere to the traditional relational schema. They are often used for applications with unstructured or semi-structured data, such as social media feeds, sensor data, and real-time analytics. Examples include MongoDB (document-oriented), Cassandra (column-family), and Redis (key-value).

- **NewSQL Databases:** These databases attempt to combine the scalability of NoSQL databases with the ACID properties of relational databases. They are designed for applications that require high performance and strong data consistency. Examples include CockroachDB and VoltDB.

Database Interactions in Web Applications:

Web applications typically interact with databases through a database access layer, which provides an abstraction over the underlying database system. This abstraction allows developers to write code that is independent of the specific database being used, making it easier to switch databases if needed.

- **Database Drivers/Connectors:** These are libraries that provide the necessary functionality to connect to a specific database. For example, psycopg2 is a popular PostgreSQL driver for Python.

- **Object-Relational Mappers (ORMs):** ORMs provide a higher-level abstraction, allowing developers to interact with databases using objects and methods instead of raw SQL queries. SQLAlchemy (as discussed previously) is a widely used ORM for Python. ORMs enhance code readability, reduce the risk of SQL injection vulnerabilities, and improve developer productivity.

CRUD Operations:

As discussed in previous responses, CRUD (Create, Read, Update, Delete) operations are fundamental to database interactions in web applications. They define the basic actions that can be performed on data stored in the database.

Real-world Scenarios:

- **E-commerce Website:** An e-commerce website uses a database to store product information, customer details, orders, and inventory. Database interactions are crucial for displaying product catalogs, processing orders, managing customer accounts, and updating inventory levels.

- **Social Media Platform:** A social media platform uses a database to store user profiles, posts, comments, and relationships between users. Database interactions are essential for displaying user feeds, posting updates, adding comments, and managing user connections.

Addressing Potential Questions:

- **Database Migrations:** As applications evolve, database schemas may need to be updated. Database migrations provide a way to manage these schema changes in a controlled and repeatable manner. Tools like Alembic (for SQLAlchemy) and Flyway (for Java) are commonly used for database migrations.

- **Database Security:** Protecting sensitive data stored in databases is crucial. Implementing proper authentication, authorization, and data encryption is essential for database security. OWASP (2021) provides valuable resources and guidelines for web application security, including database security.

- **Database Performance:** Database performance is critical for web application performance. Techniques like indexing, query optimization, and caching can be used to improve database performance.

In conclusion, databases are essential components of modern web applications, providing persistent storage and efficient access to application data. Understanding different types of databases, database interaction techniques, and best practices for database security and performance is crucial for building robust and scalable web applications.

2.1 SQLITE WITH PYTHON: DIRECT DATABASE INTERACTION

The sqlite3 library in Python offers a simple yet powerful interface for interacting with SQLite databases. As part of Python's standard library, it requires no external installations, making it readily accessible to all Python developers. This accessibility, combined with SQLite's inherent simplicity (file-based, serverless), makes it an excellent choice for various applications, particularly those requiring local data storage or rapid prototyping.

Here's a breakdown of how the sqlite3 library facilitates database interaction:

- **Connection Management:** The core of interaction begins with establishing a connection to the database file using sqlite3.connect('database_name.db'). This function returns a Connection object, which represents the active session with the database. If the specified database file doesn't exist, SQLite automatically creates it. This ease of setup is a significant advantage over client-server database systems that require separate server installations and configurations. The connection object also manages transactions, ensuring data consistency and integrity.

- **Cursor Objects:** Once a connection is established, a Cursor object is created using connection.cursor(). The cursor acts as a pointer, allowing you to execute SQL queries and fetch results. It provides methods like execute(), fetchone(), fetchall(), and fetchmany() for interacting with the database.

- **Executing SQL Queries:** The cursor.execute() method is used to execute SQL statements. This method accepts SQL queries as strings, allowing you to perform all standard SQL operations like CREATE TABLE, INSERT, SELECT, UPDATE, and DELETE. It's crucial to use parameterized queries (using placeholders like ?) to prevent SQL injection vulnerabilities, a common security threat in web applications.

- **Data Retrieval:** After executing a SELECT query, the cursor provides methods for retrieving the results. fetchone() fetches a single row, fetchall() fetches all rows, and fetchmany(size) fetches a specified number of rows. The retrieved data is typically returned as tuples, where each element in the tuple corresponds to a column in the result set.

- **Transaction Management:** The Connection object manages transactions, ensuring that database operations are performed atomically. The connection.commit() method saves changes to the database file, while connection.rollback() reverts any changes made since the last commit. This is crucial for maintaining data integrity, especially in applications that involve multiple related database operations.

- **Error Handling:** The sqlite3 library provides exceptions for handling database errors. Common exceptions include sqlite3.Error, sqlite3.OperationalError, and sqlite3.IntegrityError. Proper error handling is essential for robust application development.

- **Data Type Handling:** SQLite has a dynamic type system, meaning that data types are associated with values, not columns. However, the sqlite3 library maps Python types to SQLite types for seamless data exchange.

In summary, the sqlite3 library provides a clean and efficient way to interact with SQLite databases directly from Python. Its simplicity and integration with the standard library make it a powerful tool for various applications, from small personal projects to embedded systems and even as a backend for prototyping web applications. While it may not be suitable for extremely high-concurrency applications, its ease of use and portability make it a valuable asset in a Python developer's toolkit.

2.1.1 Connecting to the SQLite Database

First, we need to establish a connection to our database. If the database file doesn't exist, SQLite will create it automatically. Here's how:

```python
import sqlite3


def create_connection(db_file):
    """Create a database connection to the SQLite database specified by db_file."""
    conn = None
    try:
        conn = sqlite3.connect(db_file)
```

```python
        return conn
    except sqlite3.Error as e:
        print(e)
    return conn


# Example usage (in models.py):
db_path = "mydatabase.db" # Database file name
conn = create_connection(db_path)
if conn:
    print(f"Connected to database: {db_path}")
    conn.close() # Close the connection when done
else:
    print("Error connecting to database")
```

Potential Question: What if the database file is in a different directory?

Solution: You can provide the full path to the database file: db_path = "/path/to/my/database.db" or use relative paths like "./data/mydatabase.db".

2.1.2 Creating a Database Table

Now, let's define the schema for our table and create it in the database. For this example, let's create a table named tasks with columns for id, name, and description.

```python
import sqlite3


def create_table(conn, create_table_sql):
    """Create a table from the create_table_sql statement."""
    try:
        c = conn.cursor()
        c.execute(create_table_sql)
    except sqlite3.Error as e:
        print(e)


# Example usage (in models.py):
def create_tasks_table(conn):
    sql_create_tasks_table = """
        CREATE TABLE IF NOT EXISTS tasks (
            id INTEGER PRIMARY KEY AUTOINCREMENT,
```

```
        name TEXT NOT NULL,

        description TEXT

    );

    """

    if conn is not None:

        create_table(conn, sql_create_tasks_table)

    else:

        print("Error! Cannot create the database connection.")


# Example usage (in app.py or a setup script):

conn = create_connection(db_path)

if conn:

    create_tasks_table(conn)

    conn.close()
```

Explanation:

- CREATE TABLE IF NOT EXISTS tasks: This SQL statement creates a table named tasks only if it doesn't already exist.

- id INTEGER PRIMARY KEY AUTOINCREMENT: This defines an integer column named id as the primary key, automatically incrementing for each new record.

- name TEXT NOT NULL: This creates a text column named name that cannot be empty.

- description TEXT: This creates a text column named description.

Potential Question: What are other data types available in SQLite?

Solution: SQLite supports several data types, including INTEGER, TEXT, REAL (floating-point numbers), BLOB (binary large objects), and NULL.

2.2 ALTERNATIVE: SQLALCHEMY (OPTIONAL)

SQLAlchemy stands as a prominent and versatile Object-Relational Mapper (ORM) for Python, bridging the gap between object-oriented programming paradigms and relational databases. An ORM acts as an abstraction layer, allowing developers to interact with databases using Python objects and methods rather than writing raw SQL queries. This approach offers several advantages, including increased code readability, improved maintainability, reduced risk of SQL injection vulnerabilities, and database portability.

Key Concepts and Benefits:

- **Object-Relational Mapping:** At its core, SQLAlchemy maps Python classes to database tables. Each class represents a table, and each instance of the class represents a row in that table. Attributes of the class correspond to columns in the table. This mapping allows developers to manipulate database data using familiar object-oriented concepts like objects, attributes, and methods. For instance, a class User might be mapped to a table users with attributes like id, name, and email corresponding to columns in the users table.

- **Abstraction from SQL:** One of the primary benefits of using an ORM is that it abstracts away the complexities of writing raw SQL. Developers can perform database operations using Python code, and SQLAlchemy translates these operations into the appropriate SQL queries behind the scenes. This simplifies database interactions and reduces the likelihood of syntax errors and SQL injection vulnerabilities (OWASP, 2021). For example, instead of writing SELECT * FROM users WHERE name = 'John', a developer could use SQLAlchemy to write User.query.filter_by(name='John').all().

- **Database Portability:** SQLAlchemy supports a wide range of database backends, including PostgreSQL, MySQL, SQLite, and Oracle. This makes it easier to switch between databases without having to rewrite large portions of the application's data access layer. SQLAlchemy provides a consistent API regardless of the underlying database, enhancing code portability. This addresses a common challenge in software development: database vendor lock-in.

- **Two Core Components:** SQLAlchemy offers two distinct ways of working with databases: Core and ORM.

  - **SQLAlchemy Core:** This provides a SQL expression language that allows developers to write SQL queries in a Pythonic way but still gives them fine-grained control over the generated SQL.

  - **SQLAlchemy ORM:** This builds on top of Core and provides a higher-level abstraction for working with database data as Python objects. Most developers using SQLAlchemy for web applications will choose this method.

- **Real-world Scenarios:**

  - **E-commerce Platform:** An e-commerce platform could use SQLAlchemy to manage product catalogs, user accounts, orders, and inventory. Classes like Product, User, Order, and Inventory would be mapped to corresponding database tables, allowing developers to easily perform operations like adding new products, retrieving user information, processing orders, and updating inventory levels.

- o **Content Management System (CMS):** A CMS could use SQLAlchemy to manage articles, pages, users, and comments. Classes like Article, Page, User, and Comment would be mapped to database tables, simplifying the creation, retrieval, updating, and deletion of content.

- **Addressing Potential Questions:**

  - o **Performance Overhead:** Some developers worry about the performance overhead of using an ORM. While there might be a slight performance impact compared to hand-optimized SQL queries, SQLAlchemy is designed to be efficient, and the benefits in terms of development speed, maintainability, and security often outweigh the potential performance cost. Strategies like eager loading and optimized queries can further mitigate performance concerns (Sadalage & Fowler, 2012).

  - o **Learning Curve:** While SQLAlchemy has a learning curve, its well-structured documentation and active community provide ample resources for developers to learn and use the library effectively.

In conclusion, SQLAlchemy provides a powerful and flexible way to interact with databases in Python applications. Its object-relational mapping capabilities, abstraction from raw SQL, and database portability make it a valuable tool for building maintainable, secure, and efficient applications.

2.2.1 Introduction to SQLAlchemy

SQLAlchemy provides a robust and high-level abstraction layer over database interactions in Python, significantly simplifying database management and enhancing application development. By handling the intricacies of SQL queries behind the scenes, SQLAlchemy allows developers to focus on application logic rather than low-level database details. This abstraction offers several key advantages:

- **Simplified Database Interactions:** Instead of writing raw SQL queries, developers interact with databases using Python objects and methods. This object-relational mapping (ORM) approach translates Python code into SQL queries, making database operations more intuitive and Pythonic. For example, retrieving all users from a database can be achieved with a simple query like User.query.all() instead of writing SELECT * FROM users;. This simplification significantly reduces code complexity and improves readability, particularly for complex database operations involving joins, filters, and aggregations.

- **Enhanced Code Readability and Maintainability:** By abstracting away SQL, SQLAlchemy makes code more readable and easier to maintain. The code becomes more expressive and closer to the application's domain logic, making it easier for developers to understand and modify the code. This is especially beneficial in large projects with complex database schemas. For instance, defining relationships between tables (e.g., a one-to-many relationship between users and their posts) is straightforward with SQLAlchemy's relationship mapping features, making code more declarative and less verbose than equivalent SQL code.

- **Reduced Risk of SQL Injection Vulnerabilities:** SQL injection is a serious security vulnerability that occurs when user-supplied input is directly embedded into SQL queries. SQLAlchemy's parameterized queries automatically handle the proper escaping and quoting of user input, preventing SQL injection attacks (OWASP, 2021). This is a crucial security benefit, as it eliminates a common source of vulnerabilities in web applications. For instance, when filtering users by username, using User.query.filter_by(username=user_input).first() ensures that any special characters in user_input are properly escaped, preventing malicious SQL code from being injected.

- **Database Portability:** SQLAlchemy supports various database backends, including PostgreSQL, MySQL, SQLite, and Oracle. This allows developers to switch between databases with minimal code changes. SQLAlchemy's dialect system handles the specific SQL syntax and data type mappings for each database, providing a consistent API across different database systems. This is a significant advantage for applications that need to be deployed on different platforms or that may need to migrate to a different database in the future.

- **Two Levels of Abstraction:** SQLAlchemy offers two distinct ways of interacting with databases:

  - **SQLAlchemy Core:** This provides a SQL expression language that allows developers to construct SQL queries using Python expressions. While still abstracting away some low-level details, it provides more control over the generated SQL.

  - **SQLAlchemy ORM:** This builds on top of Core and provides a higher-level abstraction, allowing developers to work with database data as Python objects. This is the more commonly used approach for web applications.

- **Real-World Scenarios:**

  - **Social Networking Platform:** A social networking platform could use SQLAlchemy to manage users, posts, comments, and relationships between users. The ORM would simplify operations like retrieving a user's friends, fetching posts by a specific user, or counting the number of comments on a post.

- **E-commerce Application:** An e-commerce application could use SQLAlchemy to manage products, orders, customers, and inventory. The ORM would simplify operations like retrieving product details, processing orders, and updating inventory levels.

- **Addressing Potential Questions:**

  - **Learning Curve:** While SQLAlchemy has a learning curve, its powerful features and benefits make it a worthwhile investment. The comprehensive documentation and active community provide ample resources for learning and using the library effectively.

  - **Performance:** While there might be a slight performance overhead compared to raw SQL in some cases, SQLAlchemy is designed to be efficient, and the benefits in terms of development speed, maintainability, and security often outweigh the potential performance cost. Techniques like eager loading and query optimization can further mitigate performance concerns. (Sadalage & Fowler, 2012)

In conclusion, SQLAlchemy provides a powerful and flexible way to interact with databases in Python applications. Its high-level abstraction, enhanced security, and database portability make it a valuable tool for building robust and maintainable applications.

2.2.2 Creating Database Models (Declarative Approach)

With SQLAlchemy's declarative approach, you define database tables as Python classes:

```python
from sqlalchemy import create_engine, Column, Integer, String
from sqlalchemy.orm import declarative_base, sessionmaker


Base = declarative_base()


class Task(Base):
    __tablename__ = "tasks"

    id = Column(Integer, primary_key=True)
    name = Column(String, nullable=False)
    description = Column(String)
```

```python
# Example usage (in models.py):

engine = create_engine(f"sqlite:///{db_path}", echo=True) #
echo=True for debugging SQL

Base.metadata.create_all(engine) # Creates tables if they don't exist

Session = sessionmaker(bind=engine)

session = Session() # Create a session to interact with DB

# Example usage to add task:

new_task = Task(name="My first Task", description = "This is a
test")

session.add(new_task)

session.commit()

session.close()
```

Explanation:

- declarative_base(): Creates a base class for declarative models.

- __tablename__: Specifies the table name in the database.

- Column: Defines a column in the table with its data type and
  constraints.

- create_engine: Creates a database engine, specifying the database URL.

- Base.metadata.create_all(engine): Creates all defined tables in the database.

- Session: Factory for creating sessions to interact with database.

- session.add(): Add object to the session.

- session.commit(): Commit changes to database.

- session.close(): Close the session.

Potential Question: Why use an ORM like SQLAlchemy?

Solution: ORMs offer several advantages:

- **Abstraction:** You work with Python objects instead of raw SQL.

- **Portability:** Your code is less dependent on the specific database system.

- **Security:** ORMs help prevent SQL injection vulnerabilities.

- **Maintainability:** Code is more organized and easier to understand.

This detailed explanation should give you a solid foundation for setting up your database using both direct SQLite interaction and SQLAlchemy. In the next section, we'll implement the CRUD operations.

CHAPTER 3.

FLASK FUNDAMENTALS

3.1 ROUTING: MAPPING URLS TO FUNCTIONS

Routing in Flask is a fundamental concept that defines how web applications respond to client requests. It establishes a mapping between URL endpoints (the part of the URL after the base URL) and Python functions, determining which function should be executed when a user navigates to a specific URL. This mechanism is crucial for creating dynamic web applications that can handle various requests and deliver different content based on the URL accessed.

3.1.1 Defining URL Routes with @app.route()

The @app.route() decorator is the core of Flask routing. It associates a URL path with a function.

```python
from flask import Flask, render_template, request, redirect, url_for

app = Flask(__name__)

@app.route("/")
def index():
    return "Hello, World!"

@app.route("/about")
def about():
    return "About Us Page"
```

In this example:

- @app.route("/") maps the root URL ("/") to the index() function.

- @app.route("/about") maps the "/about" URL to the about() function.

3.1.2 HTTP Methods (GET, POST, PUT, DELETE)

HTTP methods define the type of action a client wants to perform on a resource. In CRUD operations, we primarily use:

- **GET**: Retrieve data (e.g., displaying a list of tasks).

- **POST**: Create new data (e.g., adding a new task).

- **PUT**: Update existing data (e.g., modifying a task).

- **DELETE**: Delete data (e.g., removing a task).

Flask allows you to specify the allowed HTTP methods for a route:

```
@app.route("/tasks", methods=["GET", "POST"])

def tasks():

    if request.method == "POST":

        # Handle POST request (create new task)

        pass #Implementation to be added.

    return "Tasks Page" #Handles GET requests
```

Potential Question: What happens if I try to access a route with a method that isn't allowed?

Solution: Flask will return a "405 Method Not Allowed" error.

3.1.3 URL Parameters (/<int:id>)

URL parameters allow you to capture dynamic parts of a URL and pass them as arguments to your view functions.

```
@app.route("/tasks/<int:id>")

def task_detail(id):

  return f"Task ID: {id}"
```

Here:

- /<int:id> captures an integer value from the URL and passes it as the id argument to the task_detail() function.
- The <int:> part ensures that the captured value is converted to an integer.

Potential Question: What if the user enters a non-integer value in the URL?

Solution: Flask will return a "404 Not Found" error. You can also use <string:variable_name> for string parameters.

3.2 RENDERING TEMPLATES: DYNAMIC HTML WITH JINJA2

Jinja2 is a widely used and powerful templating engine for Python that enables developers to generate dynamic HTML, XML, or other text-based formats. It provides a clean and expressive syntax for embedding Python code within template files, allowing for dynamic content generation, control flow, and data manipulation. This separation of presentation logic (in templates) from application logic (in Python code) promotes cleaner code, improved maintainability, and enhanced developer productivity.

3.2.1 Using Jinja2 Templates for HTML

Flask integrates seamlessly with Jinja2. You store your HTML templates in a templates directory within your project.

Example (templates/tasks.html):

```html
<!DOCTYPE html>
<html>
<head>
  <title>Tasks</title>
</head>
<body>
  <h1>Tasks</h1>
  <ul>
    {% for task in tasks %}
      <li>{{ task.name }} - {{ task.description }}</li>
    {% endfor %}
  </ul>
</body>
</html>
```

3.2.2 Passing Data to Templates

You can pass data from your view functions to Jinja2 templates using the render_template() function:

```
from flask import render_template
@app.route("/tasks")
def tasks():
    tasks_data = [
        {"name": "Task 1", "description": "Description 1"},
        {"name": "Task 2", "description": "Description 2"},
    ]
    return render_template("tasks.html", tasks=tasks_data)
```

In this example, the tasks_data list is passed to the tasks.html template as a variable named tasks.

3.2.3 Creating Basic HTML Forms

HTML forms are essential for creating interactive web pages. Here's a basic example:

Example (templates/create_task.html):

```html
<form method="POST">
  <label for="name">Name:</label><br>
  <input type="text" id="name" name="name"><br><br>
  <label for="description">Description:</label><br>
  <textarea                            id="description"
name="description"></textarea><br><br>
  <input type="submit" value="Submit">
</form>
```

In your Flask view function, you can access the submitted form data using request.form:

```python
@app.route("/tasks/create", methods=["GET", "POST"])
def create_task():
  if request.method == "POST":
    name = request.form["name"]
```

```
    description = request.form["description"]

    # Process the data (e.g., save to database)

    return redirect(url_for("tasks")) # Redirect to the tasks page

  return render_template("create_task.html")
```

Explanation:

- method="POST" in the <form> tag specifies that the form data will be sent using the POST method.

- name="name" and name="description" in the input fields define the names of the form fields, which are used to access the data in Flask.

- redirect(url_for("tasks")) redirects the user to the /tasks route after form submission. The url_for() function generates the URL for the given endpoint name.

Potential Question: What is url_for() and why should I use it?

Solution: url_for() generates URLs based on the function names (endpoints) you define with @app.route(). This is better than hardcoding URLs because:

- It makes your code more maintainable: If you change a URL, you only need to update the @app.route() decorator, not every instance of the URL in your code.

- It handles URL encoding and special characters automatically.

This section has provided you with the necessary Flask knowledge to create dynamic web pages and handle user interactions. In the next section, we'll integrate these concepts to implement the actual CRUD operations with the database.

CHAPTER 4.

CRUD OPERATIONS

We'll assume you have the database setup from the previous sections (either using sqlite3 directly or SQLAlchemy). We'll also assume you have basic HTML templates for displaying tasks, creating new tasks, editing tasks, and potentially a confirmation page for deletion.

4.1 CREATE: ADDING NEW TASKS

```
from flask import Flask, render_template, request, redirect, url_for
import sqlite3 # Or sqlalchemy imports

app = Flask(__name__)
# ... Database connection/setup code ...

@app.route("/tasks/create", methods=["GET", "POST"])
def create_task():
```

```python
if request.method == "POST":

    name = request.form["name"]

    description = request.form["description"]


    try:

        conn = create_connection(db_path) #Or use SQLAlchemy session

        cursor = conn.cursor() # Or use SQLAlchemy add and commit

        cursor.execute("INSERT INTO tasks (name, description) VALUES (?, ?)", (name, description))

        conn.commit()

        conn.close()

        return redirect(url_for("tasks")) # Redirect on success
    except sqlite3.Error as e:

        print(f"Database error: {e}")

        return render_template("create_task.html", error="Error creating task.") # Show error on form

    return render_template("create_task.html")
```

```
@app.route("/tasks")

def tasks():

    try:

        conn = create_connection(db_path)

        cursor = conn.cursor()

        cursor.execute("SELECT * FROM tasks")

        tasks = cursor.fetchall()

        conn.close()

        return render_template("tasks.html", tasks=tasks)

    except sqlite3.Error as e:

        print(f"Database error: {e}")

        return render_template("tasks.html", error="Error retrieving
tasks.")
```

Explanation:

- The create_task() function handles both GET (display the form) and POST (process form submission) requests.

- On POST, it retrieves the form data using request.form.

- It then inserts the data into the tasks table using an SQL INSERT statement.

- Error handling is included using a try-except block.

- After successful insertion, it redirects the user to the /tasks page using redirect(url_for("tasks")).

Potential Question: How do I handle form validation (e.g., ensuring required fields are filled)?

Solution: You can add validation logic within the create_task() function before inserting data into the database. You can use WTForms or Flask-WTF for more advanced form handling.

4.2 READ: DISPLAYING TASKS

The /tasks route, as shown in the previous example, handles reading and displaying the tasks. It retrieves all tasks from the database using a SELECT query and then renders the tasks.html template, passing the tasks data to the template.

Example (templates/tasks.html - improved):

```
<h1>Tasks</h1>
{% if error %}
<p style="color:red">{{error}}</p>
{% endif %}
<ul>
   {% for task in tasks %}
     <li><a href="{{ url_for('update_task', id=task[0]) }}">{{ task[1] }}</a> - {{ task[2] }} <a href="{{ url_for('delete_task', id=task[0]) }}">Delete</a></li>
   {% endfor %}
</ul>
<a href="{{ url_for('create_task') }}">Create New Task</a>
```

Explanation:

- Added error display.

- Added links to update and delete for each task using url_for.

Potential Question: How can I implement pagination if I have many tasks?

Solution: You can use SQL LIMIT and OFFSET clauses to retrieve tasks in batches. You would also need to add pagination controls to your template.

4.3 UPDATE: MODIFYING EXISTING TASKS

```python
@app.route("/tasks/update/<int:id>",                methods=["GET",
"POST"])

def update_task(id):

    conn = create_connection(db_path)

    cursor = conn.cursor()

    if request.method == "POST":

        name = request.form["name"]

        description = request.form"description"]

        cursor.execute("UPDATE tasks SET name = ?, description = ?
WHERE id = ?", (name, description, id))

        conn.commit()

        conn.close()

        return redirect(url_for("tasks"))

    cursor.execute("SELECT * FROM tasks WHERE id = ?", (id,))

    task = cursor.fetchone()

    conn.close()

    if task:
```

```
    return render_template("update_task.html", task=task)

return "Task not found"
```

Explanation:

- The update_task() function takes the task ID as a URL parameter.

- On GET, it retrieves the task data from the database based on the ID and renders the update_task.html template, passing the task data to pre-fill the form.

- On POST, it retrieves the updated form data and executes an SQL UPDATE statement.

4.4 DELETE: REMOVING TASKS

```python
@app.route("/tasks/delete/<int:id>")

def delete_task(id):

    conn = create_connection(db_path)

    cursor = conn.cursor()

    cursor.execute("DELETE FROM tasks WHERE id = ?", (id,))

    conn.commit()

    conn.close()

    return redirect(url_for("tasks"))
```

Explanation:

- The delete_task() function takes the task ID as a URL parameter.

- It executes an SQL DELETE statement to remove the task from the database.

- It then redirects the user back to the tasks list.

Potential Question: How can I add a confirmation dialog before deleting a task?

Solution: You can use JavaScript to display a confirmation dialog on the client-side before sending the delete request.

This comprehensive explanation should give you a strong foundation for building CRUD applications using Flask and SQLite (or SQLAlchemy). Remember to handle edge cases, implement thorough error handling, and consider security best practices for production applications.

CHAPTER 5.

ADVANCED TOPICS

(OPTIONAL)

5.1 ERROR HANDLING: GRACEFUL DEGRADATION

Proper error handling is crucial for providing a good user experience and preventing application crashes.

5.1.1 Handling Database Exceptions

We've already touched on basic error handling in the CRUD operations by using try-except blocks. Let's expand on this.

```
from flask import flash #For user feedback
import sqlite3
```

```python
@app.route("/tasks/create", methods=["GET", "POST"])

def create_task():

    if request.method == "POST":

        # ... (Get form data)

        try:

            conn = create_connection(db_path)

            cursor = conn.cursor()

            cursor.execute("INSERT INTO tasks (name, description) VALUES (?, ?)", (name, description))

            conn.commit()

            conn.close()

            flash('Task created successfully!', 'success') # Use flash for user feedback

            return redirect(url_for("tasks"))

        except sqlite3.IntegrityError as e: # Handle specific database errors

            conn.close()

            flash(f'Error: Task with this name already exists. {e}', 'error')
```

```python
        return render_template("create_task.html", error="Task
creation failed.")

    except sqlite3.Error as e:

        conn.close()

        flash(f'A database error occurred: {e}', 'error')

        return render_template("create_task.html", error="A
database error occurred.")

    except Exception as e:  # Catch all other exceptions. Important
to log this for debugging.

        print(f"Unexpected error: {e}")  # Log the full error to
console or file

        flash('An unexpected error occurred.', 'error')

        return render_template("create_task.html", error="An
unexpected error occurred.")

    return render_template("create_task.html")
```

Explanation:

- Added flash messages to provide user feedback.

- Added specific error handling for sqlite3.IntegrityError to
  handle cases such as duplicate entries.

- Added a general Exception catch-all for other unexpected errors, which is crucial for logging and debugging.

Potential Question: How do I display these flash messages in my templates?

Solution: Add the following to your base template or relevant templates:

```
{% with messages = get_flashed_messages(with_categories=true) %}
  {% if messages %}
    {% for category, message in messages %}
    <div class="alert alert-{{ category }}">{{ message }}</div>
    {% endfor %}
  {% endif %}
{% endwith %}
```

5.1.2 Implementing 404 Not Found, 500 Internal Server Error

Flask provides convenient ways to handle HTTP errors:

```python
from flask import abort


@app.errorhandler(404)

def page_not_found(e):

    return render_template("404.html"), 404


@app.errorhandler(500)

def internal_server_error(e):

    return render_template("500.html"), 500


@app.route("/tasks/<int:id>")

def task_detail(id):

    # ... (Retrieve task from database)

    if task is None:

        abort(404) # Raise a 404 error if the task is not found

    return render_template("task_detail.html", task=task)
```

Explanation:

- @app.errorhandler(404) and @app.errorhandler(500) register

  functions to handle specific HTTP error codes.

- abort(404) raises a 404 error, triggering the page_not_found()
  handler.

5.2 USER AUTHENTICATION: SECURING YOUR APPLICATION

User authentication is essential for protecting sensitive data and controlling access to certain functionalities.

5.2.1 Basic User Registration and Login

You can implement basic user authentication using libraries like Flask-Login or Flask-Security. These libraries handle user registration, login, logout, and session management.

5.2.2 Sessions and Cookies

Flask uses sessions and cookies to maintain user state between requests. Sessions store data on the server, while cookies store a session ID on the client's browser.

Potential Question: How do I protect against common web vulnerabilities like Cross-Site Scripting (XSS) and Cross-Site Request Forgery (CSRF)?

Solution:

- **XSS:** Sanitize user input before displaying it in templates using Jinja2's automatic escaping or by using a dedicated HTML sanitization library.

- **CSRF:** Use Flask-WTF, which provides CSRF protection out of the box.

5.3 RESTful APIs: Exposing Data to Other Applications

Building RESTful APIs allows other applications to interact with your data.

5.3.1 Building RESTful APIs with Flask

Flask makes it easy to create RESTful APIs using its routing and request handling capabilities.

5.3.2 Representing Data as JSON

JSON (JavaScript Object Notation) is the standard format for representing data in RESTful APIs. Flask provides the jsonify() function to convert Python data structures to JSON.

```
from flask import jsonify


@app.route("/api/tasks")
def api_tasks():
    # ... (Retrieve tasks from database)
```

```
return jsonify(tasks) # Return tasks as JSON
```

5.4 TESTING: ENSURING CODE QUALITY

Testing is crucial for ensuring code quality and preventing regressions.

5.4.1 Unit Testing Flask Applications

Unit tests test individual components of your application in isolation. You can use the unittest or pytest frameworks for unit testing Flask applications.

5.4.2 Integration Testing

Integration tests test the interaction between different components of your application. You can use tools like Flask's test client to simulate HTTP requests and test your application's behavior.

These advanced topics provide a stepping stone to building more sophisticated Flask applications. Remember that security and testing are crucial aspects of software development and should be considered from the beginning of your projects.

CHAPTER 6.

DEPLOYMENT

Deployment involves making your application available on a server, either locally for testing or on a cloud platform for public access.

6.1 DEPLOYING TO A LOCAL SERVER

6.1.1 Using flask run for Development

The simplest way to run your Flask application locally during development is using the flask run command:

```
export FLASK_APP=app.py # Set the Flask application file
export FLASK_ENV=development # Enables debug mode
flask run
```

This starts a development server that automatically reloads your application when you make changes to the code. The FLASK_ENV=development setting is crucial as it activates the debugger and other helpful development features.

Potential Question: What if my application entry point isn't named app.py?

Solution: You can use the --app option with flask run to specify the application file:

```
flask run --app my_app_module:app
```

Where my_app_module is the name of your Python file (without the .py extension), and app is the name of your Flask application instance.

6.1.2 Using a WSGI Server (e.g., Gunicorn)

For production environments, you should use a WSGI (Web Server Gateway Interface) server like Gunicorn or uWSGI. These servers are more robust and efficient than the built-in Flask development server.

To use Gunicorn:

1. Install Gunicorn:

```
pip install gunicorn
```

2. Run your application with Gunicorn:

```
gunicorn --bind 0.0.0.0:5000 app:app # Or
my_app_module:app if you have a different app name
```

--bind 0.0.0.0:5000 tells Gunicorn to listen on all network interfaces on port 5000.

Potential Question: Why do I need a WSGI server for production?

Solution: The Flask development server is not designed for handling high traffic or secure production deployments. WSGI servers like Gunicorn are designed for this purpose, providing features like process management, load balancing, and improved performance.

6.2 DEPLOYING TO A CLOUD PLATFORM

Cloud platforms offer scalable and reliable hosting for your web applications. Here's a brief overview of some popular options:

6.2.1 Deploying to Heroku

Heroku is a Platform as a Service (PaaS) that simplifies deployment.

1. Create a Heroku account and install the Heroku CLI.

2. Create a Procfile in your project root with the following content:

3. web: gunicorn app:app

4. Create a requirements.txt file listing your project dependencies:

```
pip freeze > requirements.txt
```

5. Create a Heroku app:

```
heroku create <your-app-name>
```

6. Push your code to Heroku:

```
git push heroku main
```

Heroku will automatically detect your Flask application, install the dependencies from requirements.txt, and start your application using Gunicorn.

6.2.2 Deploying to AWS (Elastic Beanstalk)

AWS Elastic Beanstalk is another PaaS offering from Amazon Web Services.

1. Create an AWS account.

2. Use the AWS Management Console or the AWS CLI to create an Elastic Beanstalk environment.

3. Upload your application code as a zip file or using Git.

Elastic Beanstalk will handle the deployment and infrastructure management.

6.2.3 Deploying to Google Cloud (App Engine or Cloud Run)

Google Cloud offers several options for deploying web applications, including App Engine and Cloud Run.

- **App Engine:** A fully managed platform for deploying web applications and APIs.

- **Cloud Run:** A serverless platform for running containerized applications.

Both offer easy deployment and automatic scaling.

General Deployment Considerations:

- **Database Migrations:** If you make changes to your database schema, you'll need to run database migrations on your production server. Tools like Alembic (for SQLAlchemy) can help manage migrations.

- **Environment Variables:** Store sensitive information like database credentials and API keys in environment variables instead of hardcoding them in your code.

- **Logging:** Implement proper logging to track errors and monitor your application's performance in production.

- **Security:** Follow security best practices, such as using HTTPS, protecting against common web vulnerabilities, and regularly updating your dependencies.

This section has provided you with an overview of deploying your Flask application to different environments. Remember to choose the deployment method that best suits your project's needs and consider the important deployment considerations to ensure a smooth and secure deployment process.

KEY CONSIDERATIONS

These considerations are not specific to a single step of the development process but rather overarching principles that should guide your entire project.

PROJECT STRUCTURE: ORGANIZATION FOR MAINTAINABILITY

A well-defined project structure is essential for maintainability, especially as your application grows in complexity. A suggested structure (building on previous examples) is:

crud_app/

├── app.py   # Main application file (Flask app initialization, routing)

├── models.py   # Database models (using SQLAlchemy or direct sqlite3)

```
├── views.py        # View functions (handling requests, interacting with models)
├── templates/      # HTML templates
│   ├── base.html   # Base template for common layout elements
│   ├── tasks.html
│   ├── create_task.html
│   ├── update_task.html
│   └── 404.html, 500.html # Error pages
├── static/         # Static files (CSS, JavaScript, images)
├── tests/          # Unit and integration tests
├── requirements.txt # Project dependencies
└── Procfile        # For Heroku deployment (if applicable)
```

Explanation:

- app.py: Contains the Flask app instance, main routes and configuration.

- models.py: Defines the database schema and interacts with the database.

- views.py: Handles user requests, interacts with the models, and renders templates. This separation of concerns (MVC -

Model-View-Controller) is a common and effective architectural pattern.

- templates/: Stores HTML templates. base.html can contain common layout elements (navigation, headers, footers) that other templates inherit from using Jinja2's template inheritance.

- static/: Stores static files like CSS, JavaScript, and images.

- tests/: Contains unit and integration tests.

- requirements.txt: Lists project dependencies for easy installation.

- Procfile: Used for Heroku deployments to specify the application entry point.

Real-world Scenario: Imagine working on a team with multiple developers. A clear project structure ensures that everyone knows where to find specific files and how to organize new code, reducing confusion and improving collaboration.

Security: Protecting Your Application and Data

Security is paramount in any web application. Here are some key security considerations:

1. Sanitize User Input to Prevent SQL Injection

SQL injection vulnerabilities occur when user-provided input is directly inserted into SQL queries, allowing attackers to execute arbitrary SQL code.

Example (Vulnerable code):

```
# DO NOT DO THIS!
task_name = request.form["name"]
query = f"SELECT * FROM tasks WHERE name = '{task_name}'"
cursor.execute(query)
```

Correct Way (Using parameterized queries):

```
task_name = request.form["name"]
cursor.execute("SELECT * FROM tasks WHERE name = ?",
(task_name,))
```

Using parameterized queries ensures that user input is treated as data, not as SQL code.

Citation: OWASP (Open Web Application Security Project) on SQL Injection: [invalid URL removed]

2. Use HTTPS for Secure Communication

HTTPS encrypts communication between the client and the server, preventing eavesdropping and data tampering.

- On local development, Flask's development server does not use HTTPS by default.
- On production, you'll need to obtain an SSL/TLS certificate from a Certificate Authority (e.g., Let's Encrypt) and

configure your web server (e.g., Nginx, Apache) or cloud platform to use HTTPS.

3. Implement Proper Authentication and Authorization

- **Authentication:** Verifying the identity of a user (e.g., login).

- **Authorization:** Determining what a user is allowed to do (e.g., access specific resources or perform certain actions).

Use strong passwords, implement password hashing (e.g., using bcrypt), and consider using multi-factor authentication for enhanced security. Libraries like Flask-Login and Flask-Security can help with authentication and authorization.

Citation: OWASP on Authentication: [invalid URL removed] (While this link is about cryptographic failures, proper authentication is closely tied to secure cryptography).

BEST PRACTICES: WRITING QUALITY CODE

Following best practices leads to more readable, maintainable, and robust code.

1. Write Clean, Well-Documented Code

- Use meaningful variable and function names.

- Write clear and concise comments to explain complex logic.

- Follow PEP 8 style guidelines for Python code.

2. Use a Version Control System (e.g., Git)

Version control allows you to track changes to your code, revert to previous versions, and collaborate effectively with others. Git is the most popular version control system.

3. Follow Security Best Practices

- Keep your dependencies up to date to patch security vulnerabilities.

- Regularly review your code for potential security issues.

- Follow the OWASP Top 10 guidelines for web application security.

Real-world Scenario: Imagine finding a bug in your application months after it was deployed. With version control, you can easily revert to a previous working version while you investigate the bug. Well-documented code will also significantly help you understand the code and fix the issue faster.

By adhering to these key considerations, you'll be well-equipped to build secure, maintainable, and scalable Flask CRUD applications. Remember that continuous learning and staying updated on security best practices are essential in the ever-evolving world of web development.

References

• Bayer, M. (2023). SQLAlchemy Documentation. https://www.sqlalchemy.org/

• Bernstein, P. A., & Newcomer, E. (1997). Principles of transaction processing. Morgan Kaufmann.

• Codd, E. F. (1970). A relational model of data for large shared data banks. *Communications of the ACM*, 13(6), 377-387.

• Garcia-Molina, H., Elmasri, R., & Keyes, J. (2002). Database system concepts. McGraw-Hill.

• Hipp, D. R. (2023). SQLite Home Page. https://www.sqlite.org/

• Kreps, J., Narkhede, N., & Rao, J. (2011). Kafka: A distributed messaging system for log processing. *Proceedings of the 3rd international conference on Networked systems design and implementation*, 1-7.

• OWASP. (2021). OWASP Top 10:2021. Open Web Application Security Project. https://owasp.org/www-project-top-ten/

• Raymond, E. S. (2003). The art of UNIX programming. Addison-Wesley Professional.

• Sadalage, P. J., & Fowler, M. (2012). NoSQL distilled: A brief guide to the emerging world of polyglot persistence. Addison-Wesley Professional.

• Silberschatz, A., Korth, H. F., & Sudarshan, S. (2010). Database system concepts. McGraw-Hill.

CITATIONS

- AWS Elastic Beanstalk documentation: https://aws.amazon.com/elasticbeanstalk/

- Flask-Login documentation: https://flask-login.readthedocs.io/en/latest/

- Flask-WTF documentation: https://flask-wtf.readthedocs.io/en/1.0.x/

- Gunicorn documentation: https://gunicorn.org/

- Heroku documentation on deploying Python applications: [invalid URL removed]

- Jinja2 documentation: https://jinja.palletsprojects.com/en/3.1.x/

- SQLite documentation on SQL syntax: https://www.sqlite.org/lang.html

This page is intentionally left blank.

ABOUT THE AUTHOR

Mark John Lado is an accomplished Information System Specialist with a strong background in education and technology. He holds a Master's degree in Information Technology from Northern Negros State College of Science and Technology and is currently pursuing his Doctorate in the same field.

Mark boasts a diverse professional experience, having served as an ICT Instructor/Coordinator at Carmen Christian School Inc., a Part-time Information Technology Instructor at the University of the Visayas, and a Faculty member at Colegio de San Antonio de Padua and Cebu Technological University. He is currently a Faculty member at the College of Technology and Engineering at Cebu Technological University.

His expertise extends beyond the classroom, encompassing Object-Oriented Programming, Teacher Mentoring, Computer Hardware, Software System Analysis, and Web Development. He actively participates in the Philippine Society of Information Technology Educators (PSITE) as a member and has contributed to the academic community through the publication of his research article, "A Wireless Digital Public Address with Voice Alarm and Text-to-speech Feature for Different Campuses," in Globus An International Journal of Management & IT.

Mark's dedication to education and passion for technology are evident in his contributions to various educational institutions, including Cebu Technological University, University of the Visayas - Danao Campus, Colegio de San Antonio de Padua, and Carmen Christian School Inc.

Biography Source:

Mark John Lado. (n.d.). *Biographies.net.* Retrieved January 24, 2025, from https://www.biographies.net/

Authors' Official Website:
https://markjohnlado.com/

This page is intentionally left blank.